THREE WINDOWS ON HEAVEN

Dear Rhonda

God Protects and helps you
for all you are doing, specially
for our country.
I present you the fruit of a
common work with eminent
international religious personalite

Cairo 12-05-2014
A. W. S.

THREE WINDOWS ON HEAVEN

Acceptance of Others, Dialogue and Peace in the
Sacred Texts of the Three Abrahamic Religions

GILGAMESH
PUBLISHING LTD

THREE WINDOWS ON HEAVEN

Published by Gilgamesh Publishing in 2013
Email: info@gilgamesh-publishing.co.uk
www.gilgamesh-publishing.co.uk

ISBN 978-1-908531-39-1

CIP Data: A catalogue for this book is
available from the British Library

TABLE OF CONTENTS

Translations of sacred texts:

Complete Jewish Bible, An English Version of the Tanakh (Old Testament) and *B'Rit Hadashah* (New Testament), 1998.

The New Testament of the Holy Bible, New International Version, 1984 and *The Jerusalem Bible*, Popular edition, 1968.

The Meaning of the Holy Qur'an, Abdullah Yusuf Aly, 1934.

Why this book?

The idea first came to me in 1995. It was around the time we officially launched our work in interfaith dialogue through the International Union for Intercultural and Interfaith Dialogue and Peace Education (ADIC). This organization, over which I now preside, was founded by the late Dr. Adel Amer, the man I consider my "mentor" in everything having to do with dialogue.

My main quest was to search for concepts common to the three Abrahamic religions. It is this quest that has guided my steps ever since.

In my capacity as advisor to the grand imam of Al-Azhar for interfaith dialogue, and as vice-president of the Permanent Committee of Al-Azhar for Dialogue with the Monotheistic Religions (presided over by Sheikh Fawzi El-Zefzaf – vice-rector of Al-Azhar) I participated in the drafting and signing of two historical agreements for Muslim-Christian dialogue.

The first was between Al-Azhar and the Vatican in 1998. This project, which I initiated with Cardinal Franz König and Grand Imam Gad el-Haq Aly Gad el-Haq, both of whom have since passed away, was given unfailing support by Pope John Paul II and Grand Imam Gad el-Haq's successor Grand Imam Mohamed Sayed Tantawi. The work of Cardinal Francis Arinze and Archbishop Michael Fitzgerald, head of the Pontifical Council for Interreligious Dialogue, was also invaluable to the success of this agreement.

In 2001, a similar agreement for dialogue between Al-Azhar and the Anglican Communion was signed by the Archbishop of Canterbury George Carey, Canon Christopher Lamb, and Bishop Mouneer Hanna Anis on behalf of the Anglican Communion; and on behalf of Al-Azhar, signed by Grand Imam Tantawi, Sheikh El-Zefzaf, and me.

It was in this context of a search for commonalities among the three Abrahamic religions that I had ongoing discussions with representatives of the Jewish religion in France, Europe, the USA and Israel.

Upon being elected president of ADIC, it was clear to me that the very name of our association implies that we must extend the dialogue to include followers of Judaism. By turning the initial accomplishment of holding Muslim-Christian dialogue into a broader one involving Muslim-Christian-Jewish dialogue, we would share in the connection that exists among the three great religions that descend directly from Abraham.

Now, in this same spirit, ADIC has taken on the additional mission of promoting dialogue between cultures, for this is another path through which we may ease and pacify relationships among followers of different religions.

However, I must admit that we, as men of dialogue, have not yet succeeded to move dialogue from the circles of the elite to the wider horizons of the masses. And yet, all holy texts encourage us to do just that.

We may sometimes wonder what would be the destiny of humanity without religion or without faith. For at their core, religions and faith are all about loving and understanding others – and what would the world be without love?

Seeking the true essence of the sacred texts of the three Abrahamic religions is therefore a must. In the Hebrew Bible, for example, a stranger is automatically awarded a special status, one that entitles him to certain treatment, one that is quite unlike the treatment that Arab Palestinians receive from some Israelis. By the same token, Muslims who espouse a sinister interpretation of the Qur'an have become a threat not only to non-Muslims but to their own co-religionists.

At times I cannot help but dwell on what my friend Theodore Klein, former president of the Representative Council of Jewish Institutions in France (CRIF), once said: "We should be wise, but we tend to forget. Everything that needs to be said is contained in that holy text, but in reality humanity is still far from achieving it."

To love God, we must love one another. We must also strive to close the gap between the three major religions of our times. Even though they all come from the same place, this can only be done if we are humble and brave enough to admit that no religion has a monopoly on faith, no religion has a monopoly on the word of God, and no religion has a monopoly on determining where one stands in the eyes of God.

Rather, we must all understand that acceptance of others, dialogue and peace, are inextricably linked. Indeed, peace, this universally shared ideal that we can live together in harmony, without animosity or war, is largely the result of well-intentioned dialogue, an individual choice to engage in mutual understanding, which must begin with acceptance of the other.

It is in the light of these three themes, and in a spirit of reconciliation, that these eminent scholars, nourished by faith and experience, have agreed to select and comment upon some passages from the Hebrew Bible, the Gospels and the Qur'an.

Speaking for myself and my colleagues in ADIC, I hope this book will illuminate the heart of Jewish, Christian and Muslim acts of faith, and help believers to know one another better in the service of peace.

Dr. Aly El-Samman

President, International Union for Intercultural and Interfaith Dialogue and Peace Education (ADIC)

Acknowledgments

I wish to express my deepest gratitude to all the people who brought this book to fruition:

Grand Mufti Aly Gomaa, who enjoys the respect and esteem of millions of Muslims, but also of non-Muslims, so deep are his science, his faith and conviction. I am profoundly grateful for his constant support and insight.

Chief Rabbi René-Samuel Sirat who honored us with his presence at the interfaith conference organized by ADIC at the Sorbonne in 1995 and who always distinguished himself by his close relationships with representatives of the other two Abrahamic communities.

Archbishop Michael Fitzgerald who worked so patiently, with Cardinal Arinze, and under the guidance of His Holiness Pope John-Paul II, for the signing of the historical agreement between Al-Azhar and the Vatican in 1998.

Rabbi Michel Serfaty, to whom, as a Muslim, I am also grateful for his having founded the Judeo-Muslim Friendship Association of France in cooperation with the Paris Mosque.

Chief Rabbi David Rosen, who enriches the international conferences in which we meet with the sharpness of his thought, the simplicity of his statements, and his openness to everyone – qualities that have won him respect at the highest levels at the Vatican and at the Church of England.

The Rev. Dr. Mouneer Hanna Anis, Egyptian bishop of the Episcopal / Anglican Diocese of Egypt with North Africa, the Horn of Africa, Jerusalem and the Middle East, was a key participant in drafting the agreement between Al-Azhar and the Anglican Communion in 2001. Bishop Anis continues, at my side, to make tireless efforts in the service of dialogue and peace.

Dr. Mahmoud Azab, advisor of the grand imam of Al-Azhar for interfaith dialogue, who I knew in Paris where he was professor of Islamic Studies at the National Institute of Eastern Languages and Civilizations (INALCO).

The late Dr. Abdel Moity Bayoumi, a devoted interfaith dialogue activist and member of Egypt's Supreme Council for Islamic Affairs, as well as of Al-Azhar's Islamic Research Academy. I was honored to collaborate with him and his contributions will be greatly missed.

Dr. Marie-Laure Mimoun-Sorel of the Australian Catholic University, who used her extensive knowledge and the language of faith to give us comments on the Gospels of the New Testament. Her work inspired His Eminence the late Franz König, former archbishop of Vienna, president of the interreligious commission at the Vatican, and honorary president of ADIC, to say: "Despite the youth of the writer, I completely agree with the entire text. I would not change a word of it."

Victoria Harper, friend and long-time associate, whose abilities and professionalism were indispensable to the realization of this book.

Dr. Aly El-Samman

Introduction

In the midst of endemic turmoil and sectarian conflict in various parts of the world, people often forget that Judaism, Christianity and Islam basically teach the same thing: that people should honor and care for one another. The sacred texts of the three major religions tracing their lineage back to Abraham are unanimous on that fact. Yet so many followers of these religions seem to have forgotten this simple truth.

Through meticulous research into the sacred texts of Judaism, Christianity and Islam, top scholars from such highly regarded institutions as the Australian Catholic University, Al-Azhar and the American Jewish Committee find clear guidance on the increasingly pressing issues of accepting others, dialogue and peace. The conclusion that emerges from these writings is that all humans, especially those professing faith in the Abrahamic religions, have a moral duty to accept and protect not only their brethren, but also those who differ from them in terms of race, culture, and creed.

Peacemakers have long expounded on the need for dialogue. And here their views are bolstered by passages from sacred texts explained by top religious experts. They agree that to respect others and work through difficult issues together is not an easy task, for it requires a great deal of humility. And yet it is in the acceptance of others and cooperation with them that our homage to Abraham's legacy is validated.

The call for compassion and commitment to peace that runs through this book is centuries old, yet it is as valid today as it was when Abraham's teachings became part of the traditions most sacred to Jews, Christians and Muslims. This call is too often drowned out by the worries and fears of modern life. So this book, written in the authoritative voice of some of the best minds in the field, is a reminder that faith is an assertion, not a negation, of a basic human equation: to accept and to be accepted is to live in peace.

In the foreword to this book, Bishop Mouneer Hanna Anis summarizes the logic of striving to accept others in a quotation from the Gospel of John: "If anyone says, 'I love

God,' yet hates his brother, he is a liar. For anyone who does not love his brother, whom he has seen, cannot love God, whom he has not seen." (1 John 4:20)

Indeed, how can we claim to love God on whom we have never laid eyes if we reject any of God's children who are right here before us?

In his preface for *Meeting the Other*, the chapter on the themes of accepting others, dialogue and peace in the Hebrew Bible, Chief Rabbi René-Samuel Sirat confirms that the biblical passages selected by the authors accurately represent a sincere Jewish hope, one that affirms "faith in a future of love shared among all fellow human beings". He adds that universal peace and fraternity depend on "the eternal values embodied by these monotheistic religions".

In *Meeting the Other*, written jointly by Rabbi Michel Serfaty and Chief Rabbi David Rosen, passages from the Hebrew Bible explain man's true dignity as originating from God himself, every man being created in His image. "Because God created every single human being in His image, concern for the welfare of all humanity is an integral part of the Jewish faith," write the authors. Since we all descend from Adam, we are all brothers and sisters, regardless of religious, cultural or racial differences.

With respect to accepting others, there is a strong streak of social justice in the Hebrew Bible. Not only is God the Creator, but He is also moral, just and righteous. His unmistakable commandment is laid down in Leviticus: "… you shall love your neighbor as yourself, I am the Lord." The same commandment applies to the stranger dwelling among the "home-born", and even enemies are to be fed and cared for.

Regarding dialogue the authors write: "True dialogue, in particular among believers, is nothing less than a religious imperative." Dialogue for the sake of peace is to follow instructions given in the Hebrew Bible not only to avoid evil and do good, but to consciously pursue peace. In fact, the Hebrew word for peace – shalom – comes from the root "shalem" meaning whole, complete, and well. Peace is all-encompassing and necessary for well being.

In the preface to *On the Road to Peace*, the chapter presenting the themes of acceptance, dialogue and peace in the Gospels, Archbishop Michael Fitzgerald explains that in the 1960s the Catholic Church officially mandated inclusiveness in its encounters and relations with other religions. In particular, the Second Vatican Council's Nostra Aetate stipulates that the Church should never reject any truth presented by other religions (NA2) and that it has profound respect for Muslims (NA3).

In this spirit, Dr. Marie-Laure Mimoun-Sorel, the author of *On the Road to Peace*, equates acceptance of others with the unconditional love taught by Jesus, and explains that forgiveness is part and parcel of unconditional love. In the gospel of Matthew Saint Peter put this question to Jesus: "Lord how many times shall I forgive my brother when he sins against me? Up to seven times?" And Jesus' answer to him: "I tell you not seven times, but seventy-seven times."

Dr. Mimoun-Sorel describes this teaching of forgiveness as a path to peace, both inner and outer: "…as true forgiveness heals scars, frees one from the past, and restores one to life," and "after accepting others… forgiving offenses, and submitting to God's will, peace comes naturally."

With regard to dialogue, she asserts that according to the Gospels, success depends greatly on faith and heart: to build constructive dialogue one must be in tune with divine will, and for communication to have an impact it must be conducted with humility. Superficial dialogue will never bear fruit. But with humility and faith in God, the obstacles set in place by pride may be overcome.

In the preface to *A Message of Unity*, the chapter illuminating the themes of acceptance of others, dialogue and peace in the Qur'an, Grand Mufti Aly Gomaa highlights the similarities among the faiths that share Abraham's lineage and finds in them a reason for cooperation. He writes: "…the elements of consensus between Islam and the other monotheistic religions are much greater than those of difference, and there is no excuse for insularity and separation."

Dr. Mahmoud Azab and Dr. Abdel Moity Bayoumi, illustrate this notion through examples from the Qur'an describing Islam's heritage of Judaism and Christianity. In fact, the Qur'an does not describe Islam as a new religion; rather it is revealed as a continuation of the religion of "the old nations", and the prophets from earlier holy books are mentioned repeatedly in this context. And one qur'anic verse, or *sura*, describes the virgin birth of Jesus as a miracle performed for one community of people holding the same belief in God.

The religious and historical connections shared by the children of Abraham are a strong foundation for dialogue. And cooperation with others to gain peace is so important that, even in the case of war, the Qur'an calls on Muslims to extend their hands to those willing to reciprocate.

As for relations among different ethnic groups, we are shown that God purposely created us different from one another so as to entice us to think, to learn, and to explore the essence of our humanity. It is a most revealing religious text about the need for dialogue to perform our duty towards God and one another, to engage in acceptance and peaceful co-existence.

Reading this book's learned interpretations of verses from the sacred texts of the three Abrahamic religions, we find a common message that runs through their broad range of teachings. This message is one of reaching out to others and recognizing their innate humanity, for to find out what is common among us is to find God.

When we accept others and learn to communicate from the heart, we truly comprehend the religious teachings that were revealed to guide us. Everything we live for, the opinions we hold, and the values we cherish. Everything we discuss when we enter into dialogue and everything we do as a result of that dialogue. All of this comes down to a simple quest: to accept others in pursuit of peace.

Dr. Aly El-Samman

Cardinal Franz König (left), member of the Sacred College of Cardinals at the Vatican, meets Grand Imam of Al-Azhar, Gad el-Haq Aly Gad el-Haq (centre) and the author (right) in Bern in 1993.

From left: Dr. Hamdy Zagzoug, dean of the Theology Department at Al-Azhar; Cardinal Franz König of Austria; the author; and René-Samuel Sirat, former chief rabbi of France at the ADIC Interfaith Conference at the Sorbonne, Paris, 1994.

Pope John Paul II thanks the author for his efforts following the creation of the Joint Committee for Dialogue between the Vatican and Al-Azhar, Vatican City, 1998

Grand Rabbi René-Samuel Sirat (centre) meets Grand Imam Mohamed Sayed Tantawi (left) and the author (right) at Al-Azhar in Cairo, 1999.

Coptic Pope Shenouda III with the author in Cairo, 2006

From left: the author with Bishop Mouneer Hanna Anis and Archbishop of Canterbury Justin Welby during his visit to All Saint's Cathedral in Cairo, 2013.

Foreword

Effective dialogue is a life-long journey in which those involved walk together with sincerity and face directly whatever weaknesses and challenges might come their way. There are many challenges that confront this journey, including how to bring the culture of dialogue and the acceptance of others to a grassroots level, and how to go from "accepting the other" to "loving the other".

Dr. Aly El-Samman, president of the International Union for Intercultural and Interfaith Dialogue and Peace Education, is achieving this effective dialogue through a "person to person" approach. As individuals from each religion engage with others through serving society, contact is established, similarities are observed and communication is enhanced.

Coming together in service is truly one of the most effective methods of dialogue, one for which the love of humankind in all its diversity is the underlying motive for participation. Joint action deepens love and connection in the doing of good deeds.

The Bible reminds us: "If anyone says, 'I love God,' yet hates his brother, he is a liar. For anyone who does not love his brother, whom he has seen, cannot love God, whom he has not seen." (1 John 4:20)

Reflecting on this reminds us that in order to love God, we must love each other. I trust that this book will deepen understanding among all people and help us all to appreciate each other as beings created intentionally by God.

Dr. Mouneer Hanna Anis

Bishop of the Episcopal / Anglican Diocese of Egypt with North Africa and the Horn of Africa

President Bishop of the Episcopal / Anglican Province of Jerusalem and the Middle East

Acceptance of Others, Dialogue and Peace in the Hebrew Bible

Preface

This excellent initiative undertaken by Dr. Aly El-Samman, the president of the International Union for Intercultural and Interfaith Dialogue and Peace Education (ADIC), presents the fundamental positions of the Abrahamic religions on themes essential to our respective faiths such as the acceptance of others, interfaith dialogue and the teaching of peace.

On June 13, 1994, Dr. El-Samman moderated an interfaith roundtable held by ADIC at the Sorbonne in which I participated with Dr. Hamdi Zagzoug, dean of the Faculty of Theology of Al-Azhar in Cairo; and the late Cardinal Franz Köenig, archbishop of Vienna. This publication is a response to the unanimous decision we made that day to "never again separate the children of Abraham".

When humanity passes through difficult times, people must vigorously remember the eternal values embodied by these monotheistic religions, as they are indispensable to universal peace and fraternity.

The biblical and rabbinic texts presented by our colleagues are an accurate and clear representation of the beliefs and convictions that Judaism is honored to have revealed to mankind. They are also the source of the Jewish hope that affirms our faith in a future of love shared among all fellow human beings.

Finally, the TaNaKh (Hebrew Bible) solemnly affirms that despite the violence, the wars, and the destruction of which humans are guilty, there will certainly come a time when according to the prophecy of Isaiah (11:9): "They shall not hurt nor destroy in all My holy mountain; for the earth shall be full of the knowledge of God, as the waters cover the sea."

René-Samuel Sirat

Former chief rabbi of France

Secretary-general of the Foundation for Interreligious and Intercultural Research and Dialogue (FIIRD), Geneva

Meeting the Other

The Holy Bible of Judaism is a collection of 39 books written in Hebrew between the 13th and 2nd century B.C. The term TaNaKh is the Jewish acrostic name for the Hebrew Bible, as it is divided into three parts: the Torah (the Pentateuch), Nevi'im (Prophets) and Khetuvim (Writings – such as the books of Psalms, Proverbs, and those of Minor Prophets).

Traditionally, only the Torah is seen as the literal word of God revealed through Moses at Mt. Sinai to the Children of Israel. As such, the Torah is considered by Jews as the divinely ordained "manual" for living in accordance with God's will for the community to be "a kingdom of priests and a holy nation." (Exodus 19:6)

The French philosopher Emmanuel Levinas described Judaism as the "humanism of *the other*", as a person's own humanity can only be discovered and understood through recognizing the humanity of others. Accordingly we find extensive teachings in the TaNaKh reflecting this spirit, highlighting the values of human dignity, respect for *the other*, and the importance of peaceful relations.

Acceptance of others

Dignity of the human being

The Torah views the dignity of the human being as emanating from God Himself. In accordance with the story of creation in Genesis (the first book of the Pentateuch or Torah) every person is seen as created in the divine image. This means that there is an inalienable sanctity and dignity in each human life.

> *And God created man in His own image, in the image*
> *of God He created him...* (Genesis 1:27)

In describing how all humanity originates from one source, the creation story conveys further moral instruction. This includes the idea of inherent human equality (all of us are children of the same parentage), as well as the fact that we are all part of one human family with a responsibility toward one another.

According to the second century Jewish sage Shimon Ben Azai, the most important precept of the Bible is found precisely in this text that summarizes the creation of the first humans:

> *This is the book of the generations of Adam (human).*
> *In the day that God created Adam, in the likeness of God*
> *He made him. Male and female He created them and*
> *He blessed them and He called their name Adam on the*
> *day He created them.* (Genesis 5: 1,2)

This awareness of being created in the divine image is what must prevent us from ever despising or humiliating another, says Ben Azai. For to do so, is ultimately to act disrespectfully toward God Himself.

The knowledge of our being created in the Divine Image should also endow us with a sense of the inestimable worth of our own lives, as well as that of others. Every individual life and each person's dignity must be respected and protected accordingly.

Above all, Jewish sages point out, this awareness should bring with it a sense of our unique human connection with the Creator. When one recognizes *the other* as part of oneself through God, one will not only reject all hatred and violence towards *the other*, but also all ideas and ideologies that stigmatize *the other*.

God Himself is the source of human equality. Once we grasp every human being's divine connection with God, respect for others is a natural result.

The story in the book of Genesis about Cain and Abel, the sons of Adam and Eve, reflects the Divine emphasis in the Torah on human relationships and responsibility one for another. When Cain murders his brother in a jealous rage, God asks him:

"Where is Abel, your brother?"

Cain denies the truth with a sarcastic reply:

"I know not. Am I my brother's keeper?" (Genesis 4:9)

God's question is not in essence an enquiry about Abel's whereabouts, but rather a reminder to Cain that Abel is his brother. As descendants of Adam, we may not ignore our responsibility for our brothers. Moreover, our responsibility to protect and care for our human brother

– especially one who has been wronged or hurt – is not mitigated by differences in religion, culture, nationality and race.

Protecting human dignity begins with respect for life. However, simply to desist from killing is not enough. Judaism urges its followers to help all who suffer or are in danger, as each one of us is "our brother's keeper".

Social justice

The Torah emphasizes that God is not just the historical creator and Lord. He is a moral God: loving, gracious, compassionate, just and righteous. Being made in the divine image thus brings with it a responsibility to live in accordance with these values – values that are the moral foundation for human society.

Human solidarity is portrayed as something that should be the natural outcome of our origins. In Judaism, the all-encompassing commandment for right action is often seen to be:

> *You shall be holy because I the Lord your God am holy.*
> (Leviticus 19:2)

Indeed the plethora of commandments that follow this injunction are primarily concerned with social justice. These values are further stressed by the biblical prophets; for example in the words of Micah:

> *It has been told to you O man, what is good and what the Lord requires of you; only to do justice and love mercy, and walk humbly with your God.* (Micah 6:8)

And in the words of Isaiah:

> *Learn to do well. Seek justice, relieve the oppressed, judge (for the cause of) the fatherless, plead for the widow.* (Isaiah 1:17)

While the abovementioned sage Ben Azai placed major emphasis on the concept of the Divine Image, his contemporary Rabbi Akiva declared that the most important principle in the Torah is the commandment:

> *...and you shall love your neighbour as yourself, I am the Lord.* (Leviticus 19:18)

Rabbi Akiva taught that not only should human solidarity flow from our awareness that we are all God's creatures and have a common origin, but even love of *the other* should flow from this and from our awareness of the Divine Presence. In other words, "Love your neighbor **who is** as yourself."

The word *hesed* comes from the root *h.s.d.* meaning *"loving kindness"*. This is the same root for the words *hasid* and *hasidut – pious and piety –* clearly associating piety with acts of loving kindness.

Hasidut was interpreted by our sages, the Talmudic[1] rabbis, as the higher law, equivalent to the modern concept of *"social equity"*. Thus Judaism teaches that piety is not piety, without justice and kindness.

The prophet Amos denounces all piety devoid of justice.

> *Take away from Me the noise of your songs; and let Me not hear the melody of your hymns. But let justice well up as waters, and righteousness as a mighty stream.* (Amos 5:23-24)

---

1. The Talmud is the primary source of Jewish religious law, consisting of the Mishnah and the Gemara.

Similarly the prophet Isaiah berates those who go through the motions of fasting without grasping the essential religious ethical purpose of it all.

> *Is this the fast that I choose, a day of man's afflicting his soul? Is it to bend his head like a fishhook and spread out sackcloth and ashes? Will you call this a fast and an acceptable day to the Lord?*
>
> *Is this not the fast I will choose? To undo the fetters of wickedness, to untie the bonds of evil, and to let out the oppressed free, and all wickedness you shall eliminate. Is it not to share your bread with the hungry...)* (Isaiah 58:5-7)

Throughout the Hebrew Bible, acts of loving kindness (*hesed*), righteousness (*tzedakah*) and compassion (*rahamim*) are presented as the very means by which Jews imitate the Divine Attributes (Imitatio Dei).

> *For I have known him because he commands his sons and his household after him, that they should keep the way of the Lord to perform righteousness and justice, in order that the Lord bring upon Abraham that which He spoke concerning him.* (Genesis 18:19)

> *He has told you, O man, what is good, and what the Lord demands of you; but to do justice, to love loving-kindness, and to walk discreetly with your God.* (Micah 6:8)

> *(…) Your father-did he not eat and drink and perform justice and righteousness? Then it was well with him. He judged the cause of the poor and needy, then it was good. Is not that the knowledge of Me? says the Lord.* (Jeremiah 22:15-16)

> *For if you keep all these commandments which I command you to do them, to love the Lord, your God, to walk in all His ways, and to cleave to Him.* (Deuteronomy 11:22)

To walk in all God's way is to fulfil the Biblical commandments through acts of justice and compassion.

Responsibility for the vulnerable

Not only are the followers of Judaism obliged to respect the life, dignity, family and property of others, the Torah is replete with injunctions concerning our responsibilities for the vulnerable: the poor, the orphan, the widow and the stranger. For example, we are required to leave part of our fields and harvest for the poor and for the non-Jews amongst us who do not have the natural family/communal support system.

> *And when you reap the harvest of your land, you shall not reap the corners of your field, nor shall you gather the gleaning of your harvest. And you shall not glean your vineyard, neither shall you gather the fallen fruit of your vineyard; you shall leave them for the poor and for the stranger.* (Leviticus 19:9-10)

The appeal to behave with compassion, especially to those who are not part of our own community, is based on an understanding of God's moral character and our obligation to emulate Him in our human world and conduct.

> *(…) for He loves the stranger, to give him bread and clothing.* (Deuteronomy 10:18)

The Pentateuch cites the duties of the Jewish people toward strangers as many as 36 times. No other commandment features so prominently in the Torah. Indeed, not only are strangers to be treated with justice, just as members of the community, they are to be protected and loved.

> *There shall be one law for the native and for the stranger who resides in your midst.* (Exodus 12:49)
>
> *And if a stranger sojourns with you in your land, you shall not do him wrong. The stranger that sojourns with you shall be unto you as the home-born among you, and you shall love him as yourself...* (Leviticus 19:33-34)

As former victims of oppression, the Jewish people are particularly warned against such conduct towards others.

> *And a stranger you shall not wrong, neither shall you oppress him; for you were strangers in the land of Egypt.* (Exodus 22:20)

The memory of persecution is repeatedly called upon to encourage empathy for the outsider.

> *And you shall not oppress a stranger, for you know the*

feelings of the stranger, since you were strangers in the land of Egypt. (Exodus 23:9)

Even the privileges of the Sabbath apply to non-Jews living in the midst of the Jewish community.

The seventh day is a Sabbath to the Lord, your God; you shall perform no labor, neither you, your son, your daughter, your manservant, your maidservant, your beast, nor your stranger who is in your cities. (Exodus 20:9)

Judaism's holy shrine, the Temple in Jerusalem, was viewed as a shrine for humanity. At its dedication, King Solomon declares:

And also the stranger who is not of your nation Israel, when he shall come from a faraway country, for your Name's sake; for they shall hear of Your great Name and of your mighty hand and of your outstretched arm – when he shall come and pray toward this house ; hear You in Heaven Your dwelling place and do according to all that the stranger calls to You for; that all the people

of the earth may know Your name, to revere You and do
as your people Israel, and that they may know that Your
Name is called upon this house which I have built. (I
Kings 8:41-43)

And the prophet Isaiah declares:

Now let not the foreigner who joined himself to the Lord,
say, "The Lord will surely separate me from His people,"
(…) and to the foreigners who join themselves to the
Lord to serve Him and to love the name of the Lord, to
be His servants. (…the Lord says:) "I will bring them to
My holy mount, and I will cause them to rejoice in My
house of prayer…for My house shall be called a house of
prayer for all peoples. (Isaiah 56:3,6-7)

The believer, regardless of creed, is entitled to
compassion and justice. These are the very pillars of Jewish
morality, the foundation on which the House of God is
built. Those who truly believe in God must be capable of
compassion and justice towards all, regardless of birthplace
or faith.

The enemy

Arguably the greatest challenge in terms of conduct towards *the other* confronts us when the latter is hostile to us and becomes our enemy.

Even though Judaism requires us to protect ourselves and our community against assault, we are warned never to forget the humanity of *the other* – even those who are our enemies.

> *If your enemy is hungry, feed him bread, and if he is thirsty, give him water to drink.* (Proverbs 25:21)
> *When your enemy falls, do not rejoice, and when he stumbles, let your heart not exult."* (Proverbs 24:17)

Similarly, the fact that someone is one's enemy does not give one license to disregard, let alone plunder, his livestock or property.

> *If you come upon your enemy's ox or his stray donkey, you shall surely return it to him. If you see the donkey of he who hates you, lying under its burden and would refrain from releasing it; You (shall not do so, but) shall surely release it with him.* (Exodus 23:4-5)

These verses make it clear that if hostility cannot be avoided, a place in one's heart must be found for compassion.

Salvation for all

Jewish understanding of the biblical narrative views all humanity as bound to God in what is known as the Noahide Covenant, established with Noah and his descendants after the great flood.

> *And I, behold I am setting up My covenant with you*
> *and with your seed after you.* (Genesis 9:9)

Jewish tradition interprets these divine commandments, or expectations of humanity, as consisting of seven universal moral principles.[2] Those who observe this universal moral code are considered in Jewish tradition to be "the righteous of the nations", who have their place in the world to come.

---

2. The moral code of the Noahide Covenant contains prohibitions against idolatry, adultery, murder, blasphemy, theft, and the eating of meat that came from an animal while it was still alive, as well as a requirement to maintain courts to enforce these laws.

Dialogue

While the Bible is replete with dialogue, the prophet Malachi appears to be the most explicit in presenting dialogue as a religious virtue:

> *Then those who revered God spoke with one another, and God listened and heard and a book of remembrance was written down before Him of those who revere the Lord and respect His Name.* (Malachi 3:16)

Malachi presents this dialogue as something notable and as giving great satisfaction to God. Moreover, one of this prophet's earlier statements is written:

> *From sunrise to its setting my Name is great among the gentiles.* (Malachi 1:11)

We see that the dialogue to which he refers is the dialogue of believers from among all nations. For the prophet Malachi, dialogue among different peoples is, in essence, an act of devotion to God.

While God is everywhere, there is only one creature that reflects the divine image and that is the human being.

Accordingly, when one who is aware of this ubiquitous divine presence approaches the other, that human encounter – that dialogue – acquires religious value in and of itself. When we respond to the divine in the other, we demonstrate reverence and respect for God Himself.

As the prophet Isaiah declares:

Seek the Lord where He may be found. (Isaiah 55:6)

True dialogue, in particular among believers, is nothing less than a religious imperative.

Peace

The essence of Torah

The Hebrew word for peace – *shalom* – comes from the root "*shalem*" meaning whole, complete, and well. Thus "*shalom*", as it is used in the Hebrew Bible, refers to complete social and spiritual well-being.

Her ways are pleasant ways and all Her paths are peace.
(Proverbs 3:17)

Accordingly, the sages of the Talmud declare that: "*the*

whole Torah is for the sake of peace" (Babylonian Talmud, Gittin 69b) and that it is this spirit that must animate all aspects of our conduct towards both Jews and Gentiles.

Conversely, it is only if we live in accordance with divine revelation that we will truly live in peace:

> *If you follow My statutes and observe My commandments and perform them, (…) you will live in security in your land. And I will grant peace in the Land, and you will lie down with no one to frighten [you]; I will remove wild beasts from the Land, and no sword will pass through your land.* (Leviticus 26:3-6)

Indeed, peace is at the heart of and is the result of all righteous conduct.

> *And the work of righteousness shall be peace; and the effect of righteousness tranquility and confidence forever.* (Isaiah 32:17)
> *Mark the man of integrity and behold the upright; for there is a future for the man of peace.* (Psalms 37:37)

The challenge – to bring peace

The quest for peace and justice is one of the most central themes in the prophetical texts. For example, God tells the prophet Zechariah:

> *Speak every man the truth with his neighbor; execute the judgment of truth and peace in your gates, and let none of you devise evil in your hearts against his neighbour; and love no false oath; for all these are things that I hate.* (Zechariah 8:16-17)

We are furthermore not only commanded to avoid all evil, but are urged to actively pursue peace.

> *Depart from evil, and do good; seek peace, and pursue it.* (Psalms 34:15)

With this verse, the sages observe that the Bible makes the goal of peace greater than the other commandments. Commandments that involve a response to another or a given situation require one to have come across particular persons and circumstances. As for peace, we are obliged to seek it and pursue it regardless of the situation. We are meant to go out of our way to advance the cause of peace.

Universal redemption

The Jewish sages declare that universal redemption will only come through peace as it is written:

> *He announces peace ... He announces salvation.* (Isaiah 52:7)

Indeed the ultimate vision of peace in the Hebrew Bible is the Messianic era where all violence and hostility is rejected.

> *And a wolf shall live with a lamb, and a leopard shall lie with a kid; and a calf and a lion cub and a fatling [shall lie] together, and a small child shall lead them. (…) They shall neither harm nor destroy on all My holy mount, for the land shall be full of knowledge of the Lord as water covers the sea bed.* (Isaiah 11:6-9)
> *And it shall be at the end of the days, that the mountain of the Lord's house shall be firmly established at the top of the mountains, and it shall be raised above the hills, and all the nations shall stream to it. (…) And*

he shall judge between the nations and reprove many
peoples, and they shall beat their swords into plowshares
and their spears into pruning hooks; nation shall not lift
the sword against nation, neither shall they learn war
anymore. (Isaiah 2:2-4)

According to these prophetic words, there will come a day when all of humankind lives in peace, a peace emanating from universal recognition of the divine presence and the divine way.

Conclusion

The essence of Judaism is that we are all the creatures of God, created in His image, and that it is our duty in this earthly life to rediscover the divine within ourselves as well as within others.

Circumstances of life, such as birthplace, background, desire and personal will, may differentiate people from each other. But if we look beneath the surface, we discover that we all share a divine bond. This is why Judaism tells us to be compassionate toward our neighbors, concerned for the less fortunate, and kind to strangers.

The Hebrew Bible offers us peace as an ideal, as something to strive for. When human history concludes, it will be at a time when this ideal is fully materialized, when all hostility has ended. This recurring refrain is best summarized in the famous line:

And the wolf shall dwell with the lamb… (Isaiah 11:6)

Until such time, we can only pursue this ideal one step at a time. We can overcome our inclinations for hostility when we recognize the same ideal in others. We can uphold human dignity by engaging in dialogue even with those who oppose us.

Because God created every single human being in His image, concern for the welfare of all humanity is an integral part of the Jewish faith.

Michel Serfaty

Rabbi of Essonne and of Ris-Orangis

Founding president, Jewish-Muslim Friendship Society of France

David Rosen

Former chief rabbi of Ireland

International director of interreligious affairs, American Jewish Committee

Acceptance of Others, Dialogue and Peace in the Gospels

Preface

In this chapter Dr. Marie-Laure Mimoun-Sorel presents the Christian approach to accepting others, dialogue and peace based on the gospels. For Christians, what Jesus is, and what he did, is as important as what he said. His being "the Word made flesh", the light that enlightens all men, as John puts it in the prologue to his gospel, and the fact that Jesus died on the cross for all people, these attest to the fundamental Christian belief in caring about others.

Following the teachings of Jesus, the First Letter of Peter gives this advice to Christians: "Always have your answer ready for people who ask you the reason for the hope that you all have. But give it with courtesy and respect and with a clear conscience." (1 Pet. 3:15-16) It must be admitted, however, that the awareness of this duty only developed gradually, and Christians have not always shown an acceptance of others.

For Roman Catholics the Second Vatican Council (1962-1965) was a turning point, and its Declaration *Nostra Aetate* (NA) on the relation of the Church to other religions has provided a sure guide for interreligious relations. This Declaration owed its origin to the desire of Pope John XXIII who convoked the Second Vatican Council to issue a statement aimed at counter-acting anti-Semitism both within the Church and throughout the world. The document stated that responsibility for the death of Jesus could not be imputed indiscriminately to all Jews, and the Church deplored all expressions of hatred and all forms of persecution against followers of the Jewish faith (NA 4).

The scope of the document was enlarged to include all religions. It underlined the fact that all human beings form one community. All are faced with the same questions and they look to different religions for answers to "the unsolved riddles of human existence" (NA 1). Special attention was given to Muslims for whom the Church expressed its esteem. Christians and Muslims were exhorted to forget the dissensions of the past, and to work together to promote social justice, moral values, peace and freedom (NA 3).

Even before this Declaration was officially promulgated, Pope Paul VI set up a special office for relations with people of other religions, the Secretariat for Non Christians, now known as the Pontifical Council for Interreligious Dialogue, an office in which I had the privilege to work from 1987 until 2006. Competence for relations with Jews was retained by the Secretariat for Christian Unity which had piloted *Nostra Aetate* through the Vatican Council. In 1974 there was established, under the Secretariat for Christian Unity, the Commission for Religious Relations with the Jews. In parallel fashion, the Commission for Religious Relations with Muslims was set up under the Secretariat for Non Christians.

The question is often raised concerning the aim of interreligious dialogue. It can be answered that there are basically three aims. The first is that people of different religions should live together in peace and harmony. The second is that they should cooperate in the service of humankind. The third is that they should encourage one another to respond according to their conscience and with greater generosity to God's call.

Encouraged by the example of the Popes Paul VI, John Paul II and Benedict XVI who were all intent upon putting into practice the teachings of the Second Vatican Council, contacts were established and formal dialogues were held with representative groups of Muslims and Jews from different parts of the world. Gradually the new attitude spread to local Catholic communities, and structures were set up to instruct Christians and to promote dialogue with people of other religions.

The Commission for Religious Relations with Jews formed a joint committee for dialogue with the International Jewish Committee for Interreligious Cooperation (IJCIC), an umbrella organisation encompassing a number of Jewish organisations. The Catholic Church has also been in formal dialogue with the Rabbinate in Jerusalem.

In a similar fashion, in order to coordinate efforts better with the Islamic community, the Pontifical Council for Interreligious Dialogue proposed setting up a joint committee with International Islamic Organisations having a religious nature. This committee was constituted on 22 June 1995, the day after the inauguration of the Mosque in Rome. It has met annually ever since.

At the constitutive meeting of this Joint Committee, two delegates from Al-Azhar Al-Sharif were present. It was decided, however, that Al-Azhar would not be part of the committee since it is not really an international organisation, but rather an Egyptian institution with an international dimension. This decision disappointed the Azharites and, thanks to the efforts and perseverance of Dr. Aly El-Samman, a special agreement was made in 1998 between the Pontifical Council for Interreligious Dialogue and the newly-created Permanent Committee of Al-Azhar for Dialogue with Monotheistic Religions. The president of this new committee was Sheikh Fawzi El-Zefzaf, vice rector of Al-Azhar; and Dr. Aly El-Samman, the grand imam's advisor for interfaith dialogue, was its vice-president. Meetings began to be held on an annual basis, alternately in Cairo and in Rome. After the pilgrimage of Pope John Paul II in the footsteps of Moses, which he undertook during the Jubilee of the Year 2000, and his visit to Al-Azhar Al-Sharif where he was so warmly welcomed, it was decided that the annual meeting would take place on or about the 24th of February, the anniversary of this visit.

While on the Pontifical Council for Interreligious Dialogue, I took part in all the meetings with the Azhar delegation, and after being appointed the Apostolic Nuncio to Egypt, I participated in the meetings held in Cairo. Our relations have always been marked by great cordiality and mutual respect. The joint committee does not produce statements of a theological nature; rather, it has made significant declarations about matters of common concern. In 1999, for instance, the committee strongly condemned the ethnic cleansing that was taking place in the Balkans, and especially in Kosovo. In 2001, it reaffirmed the special character of Jerusalem for the three monotheistic religions, and condemned the blocking of access to the Holy Places, while at the same time giving its support to efforts to find a peaceful solution to the issue of the Holy Places in Nazareth. In 2008, the committee strongly condemned the re-publication of offensive cartoons and the rising number of attacks against Islam and its Prophet, as well as other attacks against religions.

It was always emphasised that care should be taken to avoid generalisations, and that mutual respect has to be based on accurate knowledge. The committee meetings were not ends in themselves; their conclusions and resolutions needed to be communicated to the faithful of both religions. In Rome, public sessions were organised usually at the Pontifical Institute for Arabic and Islamic Studies, and the Muslim delegates were interviewed for Vatican Radio.

At the local level, dialogue continues among Christians, Jews and Muslims with varying degrees of intensity according to the different countries. Very often this dialogue is bi-lateral, but there are associations such as the Fraternité d'Abraham in France, or the Three Faiths Forum in the United Kingdom which bring together people of the three traditions. Multi-lateral dialogue also takes place as, for instance, in the movement Religions for Peace.

There is really no end to dialogue, as situations are always changing. New difficulties and new opportunities arise, making it imperative to exchange views and seek solutions together. As Pope Benedict XVI stated in an address to Muslims in Germany in August 2005: "Interreligious and intercultural dialogue between Christians and Muslims cannot be reduced to an optional extra. It is in fact a vital necessity, on which in large measure our future depends."

Archbishop Michael L. Fitzgerald
Former Apostolic Nuncio (Vatican Ambassador) to Egypt
Delegate to the Arab League

On the Road to Peace

In Latin, the word 'religion' means 'linked together'. To be religious is to be linked or connected: within oneself, to one's family, to other families, to the community, to other communities, to all human beings, to all of life, to God. The practice of religion is a means to achieve this connection, not an end in itself.

Re-connecting the individual to God, religion leads one from human love to divine love and from duality to unity, both within and without. When this unity is established, peace too is established. In this way, religions are various 'directions for use' allowing each person to reach the same aim: connection to God.

The Christian religion is known through the Gospels of Matthew, Mark, Luke, and John in the New Testament of the Holy Bible. These Gospels recount the life of Jesus and reveal his teachings. Lessons Jesus gives on acceptance of others, dialogue, and peace are part of an initiatory journey that leads his followers away from fear in all its forms to absolute and unconditional love. Through the four Gospels, Jesus' words guide the reader through her own metamorphosis. These words explain how one may awaken as a new human being, as a child of God in His own image.

As is true for the sacred scriptures of all religions, understanding the Gospels, for Christians, is an endeavor that never ends. According to progress in one's own evolution, truths are discovered that were inaccessible at previous level of awareness. At what point has one understood the Gospels and lived their teachings well enough to be able to talk and write about them? We cannot know. There is no measure by which to evaluate thoroughness of understanding or diligence of practice when it comes to the Gospels' teachings.

Professor John Ozolins of the Australian Catholic University asserts that it is not the number of classes in philosophy or degrees in religious study that makes one wiser: it is the quality of one's encounters with others and reactions to others' differences that give an indication of progress along the path towards greater wisdom. Dr Khalil

Messiha of the Coptic faith in Egypt taught that the real difficulty of this journey is not so much to know the Gospels as it is to incarnate its message.

Acceptance of Others

Human beings are not naturally tolerant. Respect for others' freedom of thinking and acting is not an automatic reflex. Acceptance of the political and religious opinions of other people is rarely anyone's spontaneous reaction. A person's natural egocentric reflex is to assess and judge others according to what one believes about himself because it is extremely difficult to see others as they really are.

According to the Gospel of Matthew, Jesus warns against such blindness:

"Why do you look at the speck of sawdust in your brother's eye and pay no attention to the plank in your own eye? How can you say to your brother, 'Let me take the speck out of your eye,' when all the time there is a plank in your own eye? You hypocrite, first take the plank out of your own eye, and then you will see clearly to remove the speck from your brother's eye." (Matthew 7:3-5)

Accepting others requires profound introspection. It is only after fully examining oneself that one is able to see others without the distortion of projection.

Born from the Spirit

In the Gospels, Jesus asks his followers to be born a second time. He explains that after being born from the flesh one must be born again from the Spirit through spiritual transformation, because the Spirit links humans to the Kingdom of God and connects them to their divine roots.

> *Now there was a man of the Pharisees named Nicodemus, a member of the Jewish ruling council. He came to Jesus at night and said, "Rabbi, we know you are a teacher who has come from God. For no one could perform the miraculous signs you are doing if God were not with him."*
>
> *In reply Jesus declared, "I tell you the truth, no one can see the kingdom of God unless he is born again."*
>
> *"How can a man be born when he is old?" Nicodemus asked. "Surely he cannot enter a second time into his mother's womb to be born!"*
>
> *Jesus answered, "I tell you the truth, no one can enter the kingdom of God unless he is born of water and the*

Spirit. Flesh gives birth to flesh, but the Spirit gives birth to spirit. You should not be surprised at my saying, 'You must be born again.' The wind blows wherever it pleases. You hear its sound, but you cannot tell where it comes from or where it is going. So it is with everyone born of the Spirit." (John 3:1-7)

Jesus provides an indispensable key when he tells his followers:

"...the kingdom of God is within you." (Luke 17:21)

If God's kingdom of love and peace is within, then it can be felt and lived. However, looking inside oneself, one finds egoism, fear, wounds, frustration, pain, and anger… but nothing of paradise regained.

Since God's kingdom is within, yet not apparent at first glance, it must be behind the fortifications of worries, judgments, and offences, of all that builds the identity. Those who embark upon a journey to reach the infinite love that lies within must travel deeper, beyond the pain that imprisons them.

Relinquishing worries

Acceptance of others begins when one gives up selfish worries. Preoccupied by the pursuit of personal interests at any price, duality is created within the self and disharmony appears in relationships.

In the Gospels, Jesus asks his followers to empty themselves of all worries, of everything that hinders them:

> *"Who of you by worrying can add a single hour to his life? (…) So do not worry, saying, 'What shall we eat?' or 'What are we to drink?' or 'What shall we wear' For the pagans run after all these things, and your heavenly Father knows that you need them. But seek first his kingdom and his righteousness, and all these things will be given to you as well."* (Matthew 6:27-33)

Worrying does not add a single hour to life and God fulfills every need. David's Psalm 23 describes the results of putting oneself in God's hands:

> *"The LORD is my shepherd, I shall not be in want."*

In other words, when God the Father leads, there is nothing to fear because although human vision is limited, God's is omniscient. Understanding this is indispensable for accepting others and engaging in harmonious dialogue.

Ceasing judgment

The ancient law of Talion "an eye for an eye, tooth for tooth" describes the law of reciprocity that rules human interaction. The Gospels suggest using acceptance as a measure of exchange, to the mutual benefit of both parties.

In the Gospel of Matthew, Jesus teaches:

> *"Don't judge, or you too will be judged; for in the same way as you judge others, you will judged, and with the measure you use, it will be measured to you."* (Matthew 7:1-2)

Jesus urges those who stand in judgment to look at themselves before judging others:

> *The teachers of the law and Pharisees brought in a woman caught in adultery. They made her stand before the group and said to Jesus, "Teacher, this woman was*

caught in the act of adultery. In the Law Moses commanded us to stone such women. Now what do you say?' (...) He looked up and said: 'if anyone of you is without sin, let him be the first to throw a stone at her.' At this, those who heard began to go away one by one at a time, the older ones first, until only Jesus was left, with the woman still standing there. (John 8:3-9)

Jesus instructs his disciples to recognize their own weaknesses in order to better understand others.

Forgiving others

Forgiving others is essential to Jesus' teaching because forgiveness has the power to bring inner peace. When individuals relate to one another through giving and taking offense, everyone suffers. The offender suffers from feelings of remorse or guilt, while the one who takes offence suffers from resentment, perhaps even the desire to take revenge. The result is that neither experience inner peace.

Jesus taught his followers to ask for God's forgiveness by praying: *"forgive us our trespasses!"* (Matthew 6:12) and reminded his disciples of their responsibility to treat others in the same way they wish to be treated:

"So in everything, do to others what you would have them do to you, for this sums up the Law and the Prophets." (Matthew 7:12)

In the Gospel of Matthew, Jesus emphasizes the importance of forgiveness:

Then Peter came to Jesus and asked, "Lord how many times shall I forgive my brother when he sins against me? Up to seven times?" Jesus answered, "I tell you not seven times, but seventy-seven times." (Matthew 18:21-22)

Here, Jesus teaches that one must forgive seventy-seven times to be free from the suffering that comes with feeling offended. The act of forgiveness is essential for healing and inner peace, as true forgiveness heals scars, frees one from the past, and restores one to life.

In The Gospel of Luke, Jesus uses the parable of the prodigal son:

Jesus continued: "There was a man who had two sons. The younger one said to his father, 'Father, give me my share of the estate.' So he divided his property between them.

"Not long after that, the younger son got together all he had, set off for a distant country and there squandered his wealth in wild living. After he had spent everything, there was a severe famine in that whole country, and he began to be in need. So he went and hired himself out to a citizen of that country, who sent him to his fields to feed pigs. He longed to fill his stomach with the pods that the pigs were eating, but no one gave him anything.

"When he came to his senses, he said, 'How many of my father's hired men have food to spare, and here I am starving to death! I will set out and go back to my father and say to him: Father, I have sinned against heaven and against you. I am no longer worthy to be called your son; make me like one of your hired men.' So he got up and went to his father.

"But while he was still a long way off, his father saw him and was filled with compassion for him; he ran to his son, threw his arms around him and kissed him.

"The son said to him, 'Father, I have sinned against heaven and against you. I am no longer worthy to be called your son.'

"But the father said to his servants, 'Quick! Bring the best robe and put it on him. Put a ring on his finger and

sandals on his feet. Bring the fattened calf and kill it. Let's have a feast and celebrate. For this son of mine was dead and is alive again; he was lost and is found.' So they began to celebrate.

"Meanwhile, the older son was in the field. When he came near the house, he heard music and dancing. So he called one of the servants and asked him what was going on. 'Your brother has come,' he replied, 'and your father has killed the fattened calf because he has him back safe and sound.'

"The older brother became angry and refused to go in. So his father went out and pleaded with him. But he answered his father, 'Look! All these years I've been slaving for you and never disobeyed your orders. Yet you never gave me even a young goat so I could celebrate with my friends. But when this son of yours who has squandered your property with prostitutes comes home, you kill the fattened calf for him!'

"'My son,' the father said, 'you are always with me, and everything I have is yours. But we had to celebrate and be glad, because this brother of yours was dead and is alive again; he was lost and is found.'" (Luke 15: 11-32)

This parable shows that when one truly accepts others, one no longer takes offence. Feeling offended is possible only if one has reduced everything around him to his own point of view. If someone rejects other ways of thinking and seeing, she rejects the identity of others. The journey towards acceptance requires that one refrain from taking offence by remaining open to other points of view and different ways of life.

The Gospels teach that God's love cannot be accessed as long as one has unresolved issues with others:

> *"Therefore, if you are offering your gift at the altar and there remember that your brother has something against you, leave your gift there in front of the altar. First go and be reconciled to your brother; then come back and offer your gift."* (Matthew 5:23-24)

Forgiveness frees a person. It gives him access to love, understanding and peace and therefore allows him to make good decisions and take the right actions.

Seeing God in ourselves

Since God revealed that man was created in His own image

it stands to reason that people would more easily accept one another and feel infinite love towards all of humanity. Why then is it so difficult for people to demonstrate their likeness to God? It is because they do not actually see the image of God in themselves and others.

It is written in the Old Testament:

> *So God created man in his own image, in the image of God he created him; male and female he created them.*
> (Genesis 1:27)

When someone says: "I believe in God," they usually mean, "I accept God without understanding Him. I believe in Him but do not see Him in me."

The Gospels teach that to be satisfied with the mere belief in God is to live in fantasy, not in God's reality. By asking his followers to walk the path towards God, Jesus asks them to become, as he did, one of God's children in God's own image:

> *"...As the father has sent me, I am sending you."* (John 20:21)

In this explanation of his role in continuing the Abrahamic tradition, Jesus describes his commitment to God's reality

> *"Do not think that I have come to abolish the Law or the Prophets; I have not come to abolish them but to fulfill them. I tell you the truth, until heaven and earth disappear, not the smallest letter, not the least stroke of a pen, will by any means disappear from the Law until everything is accomplished."* (Matthew 5:17-18)

Through the example of his own life, Jesus demonstrates that to 'accomplish' the will of God one must go beyond intellectual understanding into action.

Embodying unconditional love

Unconditional love can only be embodied when one has ceased to worry, is no longer influenced by judgment, and has forgiven all trespasses. Without this sort of deep introspective work one is not truly able to love.

In the Gospels, Jesus explains how to achieve unconditional love:

1. Love others without limit:

"Love each other as I have loved you." (John 15:12)

Love for one's neighbor should be as unlimited as Jesus' love is infinite. Yet, Jesus warns his disciples of the difficulties they will face after he is gone, and explains that he will return.

"I have told you these things, so that in me you may have peace. In this world you will have trouble. But take heart! I have overcome the world." (John 16:33)

It is understood that when Jesus rises from the dead, the love within him is resurrected as well. Nothing can ever destroy his love for all mankind.

2. Love one's neighbor as oneself:

One of the teachers of the law came and heard them debating. Noticing that Jesus had given them a good answer, he asked him, "Of all the commandments, which is the most important?"

"The most important one," answered Jesus, "is this: 'Hear, O Israel, the Lord our God, the Lord is one. Love the Lord your God with all your heart and with all your soul and with all your mind and with all your strength. The second is this: 'Love your neighbour as yourself.' There is no commandment greater than these." (Mark 12:28-31)

By giving these two commandments the same degree of importance, Jesus indicates that love for God is valid only if one also loves one's neighbour as oneself.

3. Recognize every person as a neighbour:

Jesus clarifies who should be considered a neighbour in his parable about the Good Samaritan.

On one occasion an expert in the law stood up to test Jesus. "Teacher," he asked, "What must I do to inherit eternal life?"

"What is written in the Law?" he replied. "How do you read it?"

He answered: "'Love the Lord your God with all your heart and with all your soul and with all your strength and with all your mind'; and, 'Love your neighbour as yourself.'"

"You have answered correctly," Jesus replied. "Do this and you will live."

But he wanted to justify himself, so he asked Jesus: "And who is my neighbour?"

In reply Jesus said: "A man was going down from Jerusalem to Jericho, when he fell into the hands of robbers. They stripped him of his clothes, beat him and went away, leaving him half dead. A priest happened to be going down the same road, and when he saw the man, he passed by on the other side. So too, a Levite, when he came to the place and saw him, passed by on the other side. But a Samaritan, as he travelled, came where the man was; and when he saw him, he took pity on him. He went to him and bandaged his wounds, pouring on oil and wine. Then he put the man on his own donkey, took him to an inn and took care of him. The next day he took out two silver coins and gave them to the innkeeper. 'Look after him,' he said, 'and when I return, I will reimburse you for any extra expense you may have.'

"Which of these three do you think was a neighbour to the man who fell into the hands of robbers?"

The expert in the law replied: "The one who had mercy on him." Jesus told him: "Go and do likewise." (Luke 10:25-37)

The Samaritan is a foreigner in this land, and yet he does not choose to leave this man to fend for himself. The Samaritan does not think in terms of race, religion or social class. He acts spontaneously because a life must be saved even if the man is not one of his people. He looks after the man as he would look after himself.

Reciprocally, the one rescued will love this new "neighbour" spontaneously for he owes him his life. As he realizes that the other's mercy saved him, he himself will be more likely to be merciful in the future. In this way, love and mercy are contagious, so Jesus tells his people to spread mercy like the Samaritan.

But Jesus asks even more. He asks that his followers be as free as this Samaritan, as free as this man who does not expect gratitude, but who is merciful simply because he embodies true love that does not require allegiance.

4. Love others exactly as they are:

"You have heard that it was said, 'Eye for eye, and tooth for tooth.' But I tell you, do not resist an evil person. If someone strikes you on the right cheek, turn to him the other also. And if someone wants to sue you and take your tunic, let him have your cloak as well. If someone forces you to go one mile, go with him two miles. Give to the one who asks you, and do not turn away from the one who wants to borrow from you." (Matthew 5, 38-42)

Jesus exhorts his followers to cease being at war with life, to cease rejecting others and the challenges they present. By loving another just the way he is – aggressor, thief, poor – one restores his human dignity. Generosity and love awaken the other to another expression of life, to another consciousness, another dimension. As for the one who successfully puts unconditional love to the test, she finds herself at peace.

5. Love one's enemies:

Jesus taught that to love perfectly as the heavenly Father loves, one must go beyond all limitations.

"You have heard that it was said, 'love your neighbour and hate your enemy.' But I tell you: Love your enemies and pray for those who persecute you that you may be sons of your Father in the heaven. He causes his sun to rise on the evil and the good, and send rain on the righteous and the unrighteous. If you love those who love you, what reward will you get? (…) And if you greet only your brothers, what are you doing more than others? Do not even pagans do that? Be perfect, therefore, as your heavenly Father is perfect." (Matthew 5:43-48)

"Do to others as you would have them do to you. If you love those who love you, what credit is that to you? Even sinners do that. And if you lend to those from whom you expect repayment, what credit is that to you? Even sinners lend to sinners, expecting to be repaid in full. But love your enemies, do good to them, and lend to them without expecting anything back. Then your reward will be great and you will be sons of the Most High, because he is kind to the ungrateful and wicked. Be merciful, just as your Father is merciful." (Luke 6:31-36)

In the Gospels, acceptance of others is but the first step

towards God's kingdom. Jesus taught that acceptance leads to understanding, which in turn, opens mankind to even greater love. Jesus asked his disciples to be more like the heavenly Father by overcoming their limitations and continually expanding their capacity for mercy. He called for their love to become as great as God's divine love.

Dialogue

In the Gospels, dialogue is not a simple exchange of opinion; it is a personal commitment. Jesus teaches that dialogue must be heart to heart and will be constructive only if the participants align themselves with the will of God and succeed in empathizing with one another.

Thy will be done

In the Gospel of Matthew, Jesus teaches his disciples to follow God's will:

> *This, then, is how you should pray: Our father in the heaven, hallowed be your name, your kingdom come, your will be done, on earth as it is in heaven.* (Matthew 6:9-10)

God's vision is infinite, whereas human vision is limited to the degree of openness to God's will. Jesus explains:

> *"You judge by human standards: I pass judgment on no-one. But if I do judge, my decisions are right, because I am not alone. I stand with the Father, who sent me."*
> (John 8:15-16)

Jesus urges his followers to trust in God as he is trusting in God.

Seeking clarity

In the Gospels, Jesus shows that it is necessary to be clear within oneself before entering into dialogue:

> *"Simply let your 'Yes' be 'Yes', and your 'No', 'No'; anything beyond this comes from the evil one."*
> (Matthew 5:37)

The "evil one", which can be seen here as the ego, never has pure vision. The action of the "evil one" is to oppose, to judge, to intercept, and to wish to stand alone. It believes itself to be stronger than all others. These limitations encourage the illusion that one is "king of the world", but in truth, the world does not revolve around any one person. Everyone, without exception, is carried along by the world.

Jesus warns his followers not to mistake their real aim:

> *"What good is it for a man to gain the whole world, and yet lose or forfeit his very self?"*(Luke 9:25)

The real aim -- the one that brings peace – is to find and maintain the inner clarity that keeps one's 'very self' intact. And as a result of that inner order and pure intention, one is able to produce a direct and unconditional yes or no when dialoging with others.

Dialogue and humility

The Gospels insist that dialogue must not be artificial. To engage in real communion with others, self-sacrifice is required:

> *"Now that I, your Lord and Teacher, have washed your feet, you also should do as I have done for you. I tell you the truth, no servant is greater than his master, nor is a messenger greater than the one who sent him. Now that*

you know these things, you will be blessed if you do them." (John 13:14-17)

By setting this example, Jesus shows his followers that through humility, one is able to truly communicate with others. If he, the Lord, chooses to wash the feet of his servants, then his followers should, at the very least, be willing to engage with others and interact with simplicity. Without this level of commitment, dialogue is superficial and barren.

In the Gospels, Jesus demonstrates the importance of overcoming the limitations of one's pride through dialogue with those who are different:

> *While Jesus was having dinner at Matthew's house, many tax collectors and "sinners" came and ate with him and his disciples. When the Pharisees saw this, they asked his disciples, "Why does your teacher eat with tax collectors and 'sinners'?" On hearing this, Jesus said, "It is not the healthy who need a doctor, but the sick. But go and learn what this means: 'I desire mercy, not sacrifice. For I have not come to call the righteous, but sinners."* (Matthew 9:10-13)

Jesus offers himself in service; he does not stand on a pedestal. Sharing his life with people who lead lives of sin, he is able to understand them, dialogue with them and respond to their needs.

Seeing oneself in others

In the Gospel of Matthew, Jesus affirms that empathy is the foundation for dialogue:

> *"So in everything, do to others what you would have them do to you, for this sums up the Law and the Prophets."* (Matthew 7: 12)

What people most desire from others is to be accepted. Everyone has a past, has unachieved dreams, has made mistakes, and has suffered. Recognizing these similarities and transcending differences is the key to empathy.

By connecting to God and with others, one lets go of worries, judgments, and offenses. United by a fundamental desire to live according to God's will, dialogue becomes harmonious because everyone is moving towards the same goal.

Peace

Peace cannot be forced, cannot be bought, and requires no concessions. Peace only comes from the inner unity that results from deep introspection. After accepting others, abandoning worries and judgment, forgiving offences, and submitting to God's will, peace comes naturally.

In the parable of the farmer, Jesus invites his followers to stay vigilant along the journey towards peace:

> *"A farmer went out to sow his seed. As he was scattering the seed, some fell along the path; it was trampled on, and the birds of the air ate it up. Some fell on rock, and when it came up, the plants withered because they had no moisture. Other seed fell among thorns, which grew up with it and choked the plants. Still other seed fell on good soil. It came up and yielded a crop, a hundred times more than was sown."*
>
> *"This is the meaning of the parable: The seed is the word of God. Those along the path are the ones who hear, and then the devil comes and takes away the word from their hearts, so that they may not believe and be saved. Those on the rock are the ones who receive the word with joy when they hear it, but they have no root.*

They believe for a while, but in the time of testing they fall away. The seed that fell among thorns stands for those who hear, but as they go on their way they are choked by life's worries, riches and pleasures, and they do not mature. But the seed on good soil stands for those with a noble and good heart, who hear the word, retain it, and by persevering produce a crop." (Luke 8:5-15)

To reap the fruits of peace is the aim of Christianity:

"Blessed are the peacemakers, for they will be called sons of God." (Matthew 5:9)

It is from this state of 'being in peace' that the individual is called to do greater deeds:

Again Jesus said, "Peace be with you! As the Father has sent me, I am sending you." (John 20:21)

Through the life of Jesus, as depicted in the Gospels, God shows the path that re-connects each person to Him, is a path leading from the acceptance of others to absolute peace.

Open Conclusion

This chapter, regarding the notions of acceptance of others, dialogue, and peace in the Gospels, is not an end in itself. It represents an open door for establishing an ethic of understanding among people of different religions. As Edgar Morin suggests in his philosophical works, and as Dr. Aly El-Samman practices in his work with interfaith dialogue: acceptance of others, dialogue, and peace are valid models of interaction, particularly when accompanied by a generosity of heart that leads to the exploration of one's very being, and the will to connect to that which creates identity and values.

Dr. Marie-Laure Mimoun-Sorel

Australian Catholic University

Acceptance of Others,
Dialogue and Peace
in the Qur'an

Preface

The important chapter before us presents the three themes of accepting others, dialogue and peace in the Qur'an. To illustrate these values, to make them as clear as the sun, relevant verses are included and explained.

The Qur'an provides rules for the human family and describes unambiguously that all people were created from the same man. Great emphasis is placed on this common origin of humanity. Through the Qur'an, God said:

> O mankind! reverence your Guardian-Lord, who created you from a single person, created, of like nature, His mate, and from them twain scattered (like seeds) countless men and women;- reverence Allah, through whom ye demand your mutual (rights), and (reverence)

the wombs (That bore you): for Allah ever watches over you. (An-Nisa' "The Women" 4:1)

And according to the Hadith,[3] Prophet Mohamed (pbuh) said:

You are sons of Adam, and Adam came from dust.[4]

So in the eyes of Islam, everyone, without exception, has the right to live in dignity and is expected to act with the common good and best interest of all people in mind. The differences among individuals concerning color, race, language and religion are a call for people to become acquainted with one another, not an invitation to discord or enmity:

O mankind! We created you from a single (pair) of a male and a female, and made you into nations and tribes, that ye may know each other (not that ye may despise (each other)... (Al-Hujurat "The Apartments" 49:13)

3. Hadith, in Islamic terminology, are reports of statements or actions of Prophet Mohamed, or of his tacit approval or criticism of something said or done in his presence.
4. Sunan Abu Dawud, Book 41, Number 5097.

God evaluates people according to their righteousness, which is a measure of their behavior towards others:

> ...Verily the most honoured of you in the sight of Allah
> is (he who is) the most righteous of you. And Allah has
> full knowledge and is well acquainted (with all things).
> (Al-Hujurat "The Apartments" 49:13)

In alignment with these principles, Islam defines its relationship with non-Muslims – in particular, the "People of the Book"[5] – as one based on integration and cooperation, especially with respect to the common values and ethics promoted by all religions.

Islam's approach to treating non-Muslims fairly and humanely is summarized as follows:

> Allah forbids you not, with regard to those who fight you
> not for (your) Faith nor drive you out of your homes,
> from dealing kindly and justly with them: for Allah

---

5. "People of the Book" is a term used to designate non-Muslim members of faiths which have a revealed scripture. The three types of adherents to faiths that the Qur'an mentions as people of the book are the Jews, the Sabians and the Christians.

loveth those who are just. (Al-Mumtahanah "The Woman who is Examined" 60:8)

In many such verses, the Qur'an presents the basic concepts to be taken into consideration when dealing with others. These stress the value of tolerance, which is closely related to forgiveness, and emphasize overlooking mistakes, treating people with kindness and doing good deeds.

The tolerance that Muslims show to others is due primarily to the ideas and facts instilled by Islam in their hearts and minds. Among the most important of these ideas, repeated often in the Qur'an, is that all human beings are honoured by God and the differences in religion existing among them are fundamental to God's will. Therefore, Muslims are taught neither to judge others nor to force them to abandon their faith or violate their religion.

When we examine the brilliant history of Islamic civilisation, we find that it is characterised by tolerance and mercy. This indicates that Islam, as a religion, promotes mercy and forgiveness to the highest degree, as tolerance is the fruit of faith and is the quality of those who seek not the riches of this world, but who simply desire to be closer to God.

If we accept the principles of accepting others, dialogue and peace, we recognize the value of this chapter in which the spirit of tolerance, respect, and kindness prevails. Here it is demonstrated beyond any doubt that the elements of consensus between Islam and the other monotheistic religions are much greater than those of difference, and that there is no excuse for insularity and separation.

The logical choice is for all people to live together on this earth and to build the foundations for dialogue, as willed by God Almighty. The Holy Quran and other sacred scriptures confirm that all religions share two very important values: namely, the love of God and love of neighbours. This is the essence of what is called coming to "common terms":

> *Say: "O People of the Book! come to common terms as between us and you: That we worship none but Allah; that we associate no partners with him; that we erect not, from among ourselves, Lords and patrons other than Allah." If then they turn back, say ye: "Bear witness that we (at least) are Muslims (bowing to Allah's Will).* (Al-'Imran "The Family of Amran" 3:64)

I pray to God that the author is rewarded for his clarity of vision and that the reader takes practical benefit from these words.

Dr. Aly Gomaa
Grand mufti of the Arab Republic of Egypt

A Message of Unity

Throughout the history of humankind, acceptance of others, dialogue and peace have been vital to the co-existence of different faiths. The Holy Qur'an, which is the foundation of Islam and the primary reference for all Muslims, delves deeply into these notions and describes them at length throughout the holy text.

A reader of the Qur'an will not always find the exact same words with the identical meanings they have today. But their significance as understood at the time of the revelation of the Qur'an fourteen centuries ago are not only included in the text, they shape the principal themes. Before presenting examples of these, it is useful to examine the Arabic words for "religion" and "Islam", as well as the relationship among the monotheistic religions.

Meanings of the words "religion" and "Islam" in Arabic

In the Arabic language, the word "religion" or "deen" is derived from the verb's three letter root *dan*. It is transitive and varies in connotation according to the preposition that comes after it. The range of meanings include: to be obedient, to submit, to be led, to own, to believe, and to follow. In the terminology of Islamic scholars, the word "religion" specifically means submission to God and the following of His rules, as it is God's divine guidance that leads us to the truth within belief, and teaches us to perform good deeds and to be kind to others.

As for the word "Islam" in Arabic, it comes from the verb "aslama", which means "to surrender" (to surrender oneself to God). In the Qur'an, the word "Islam" is not used to refer to a specific religion, rather it is the name of the common religion followed by all prophets throughout history and adopted by their followers. In other words, the message of Mohamed came to confirm and refine this common religion.

Relationship among monotheistic religions from Islamic perspective

When the Qur'an was revealed to Mohamed, Islam was not described as a new religion; rather it was portrayed as the religion of the prophets and the old nations:

The same religion has He established for you as that which He enjoined on Noah — that which We have sent by inspiration to thee — and that which We enjoined on Abraham, Moses, and Jesus: Namely, that ye should remain steadfast in religion, and make no divisions therein: to those who worship other things than Allah, hard is the (way) to which thou callest them. Allah chooses to Himself those whom He pleases, and guides to Himself those who turn (to Him). (Ash-Shura "Counsel" 42:13)

Even before the Qur'an was revealed to Mohamed, the People of the Book (Jews and Christians) were already surrendering to God, which is, by definition, the practice of Islam. God gives the historical account of Moses speaking to the Israelites:

Moses said: "O my people! If ye do (really) believe in Allah, then in Him put your trust if ye submit (your will to His)." (Yunus "Jonas" 10:84)

Therefore, those early believers were considered 'Muslims', even before Mohamed was born. Jesus' disciples confirm this in the Qur'an:

When Jesus found Unbelief on their part He said: "Who
will be My helpers to (the work of) Allah?" Said the
disciples: "We are Allah's helpers: We believe in Allah,
and do thou bear witness that we are Muslims. (Al-
'Imran "The Family of Al-Imran" 3:52)

And when the People of the Book heard the Qur'an, they
recognized that it was of their same religion:

And when it is recited to them, they say: "We believe
therein, for it is the Truth from our Lord: indeed we have
been Muslims (bowing to Allah's Will) from before this.
(Al-Qasas "The Narrative" 28:53)

Islam is depicted as an inseparable continuum of the other
monotheistic religions and the prophets from earlier holy
books are described repeatedly in this context:

Say: "We believe in Allah, and in what has been revealed
to us and what was revealed to Abraham, Isma'il, Isaac,
Jacob, and the Tribes, and in (the Books) given to Moses,
Jesus, and the prophets, from their Lord: We make no
distinction between one and another among them, and

to Allah do we bow our will (in Islam)." (Al-'Imran "The Family of Al-Imran" 3:84)

Islam requires complete faith in everything that comes from God as part of one's submission to Him:

And they have been commanded no more than this: To worship Allah, offering Him sincere devotion, being true (in faith); to establish regular prayer; and to practise regular charity; and that is the Religion Right and Straight. (Al-Bayyinah "The Clear Evidence" 98:5)

This faith extends to all of the prophets, regardless of their denomination, and all of the holy books regardless of language, place, or time. The Qur'an explains that each prophet had a covenant with God that bound him to the belief of all others who came with the same message:

Behold! Allah took the covenant of the prophets, saying: "I give you a Book and Wisdom; then comes to you a messenger, confirming what is with you; do ye believe in him and render him help." Allah said: "Do ye agree, and take this my Covenant as binding on you?" They said:

"We agree." He said: "Then bear witness, and I am with you among the witnesses." (Al-'Imran "The Family of Amran" 3:81)

The Qur'an describes the virgin birth of Jesus and explains that this miracle was performed for one community of people, all sharing the same belief in God:

And (remember) her who guarded her chastity: We breathed into her of Our spirit, and We made her and her son a sign for all peoples. Verily, this brotherhood of yours is a single brotherhood, and I am your Lord and Cherisher: therefore serve Me (and no other). (Al-Anbiya' "The Prophets" 21: 91-92)

Noah uses the word 'Islam' as a synonym for submitting to God's will as he urges his people to join him in preparing for the flood:

But if ye turn back, (consider): no reward have I asked of you: my reward is only due from Allah, and I have been commanded to be of those who submit to Allah's will (in Islam). (Yunus "Jonas" 10:72)

The Qur'an describes Abraham's legacy as his faith in Islam, or submission to God's will:

And this was the legacy that Abraham left to his sons, and so did Jacob; "Oh my sons! God hath chosen the Faith for you; then die not except in the Faith of Islam (Al-Baqarah "The Cow" 2:132)

On Jacob's deathbed, his sons assure him that they will put their faith in the one God:

Were ye witnesses when death appeared before Jacob? Behold, he said to his sons: "What will ye worship after me?" They said: "We shall worship Thy god and the god of thy fathers, of Abraham, Isma'il and Isaac,- the one (True) Allah: To Him we bow (in Islam)." (Al-Baqarah "The Cow" 2:133)

God describes Prophet Mohamed's relationship to all the earlier prophets as one of continuity:

And We sent, following in their footsteps, Jesus, the son of Mary, confirming that which came before him in the

Torah; and We gave him the Gospel, in which was guidance and light and confirming that which preceded it of the Torah as guidance and instruction for the righteous. (Al-Ma'idah "The Food" 5:46)

Prophet Mohamed was sent to confirm the truth of the prophets who came before him:

Nay! he has come with the (very) Truth, and he confirms (the Message of) the messengers (before him). (As-Saffat "Those Ranging in Ranks" 37:37)

And every previous book inspired by God – the Torah (from Moses) and the Gospel (from Jesus) – are in harmony with the Qur'an as guides to humankind:

It is He Who sent down to thee (step by step), in truth, the Book, confirming what went before it; and He sent down the Law (of Moses) and the Gospel (of Jesus) before this, as a guide to mankind, and He sent down the criterion (of judgment between right and wrong). (Al-'Imran "The Family of Amran" 3:3)

However, it is an over-simplification to view this harmonious relationship among the holy books as a situation in which the more recent texts confirm the more ancient by repeating the same information without modifications. Changes were made with each message and with each new book.

For example, in a description of the message that God sent Jesus to deliver, the Qur'an describes the New Testament as both maintaining and modifying laws from the Old Testament:

> "(I have come to you), to attest the Law which was before me. And to make lawful to you part of what was (Before) forbidden to you; I have come to you with a Sign from your Lord. So fear God, and obey me" (Al-'Imran "The Family of Amran" 3:50)

The Qur'an, in turn, brought modifications to certain Old and New Testament laws. Mohamed made these adjustments in accordance with God's words as they came to him in the Qur'an:

> "Those who follow the messenger, the unlettered Prophet, whom they find mentioned in their own (scriptures),- in

the law and the Gospel;- for he commands them what is just and forbids them what is evil; he allows them as lawful what is good (and pure) and prohibits them from what is bad (and impure); He releases them from their heavy burdens and from the yokes that are upon them. So it is those who believe in him, honour him, help him, and follow the light which is sent down with him,- it is they who will prosper. (Al-A'raf "The Elevated Places" 7:157).

Islam does not consider the modification of a law from another holy book as a cancellation or invalidation. Rather, modification is seen as providing continuity and relevance by allowing for flexibility without abandoning tradition:

None of Our revelations do We abrogate or cause to be forgotten, but We substitute something better or similar: Knowest thou not that Allah Hath power over all things? (Al-Baqarah "The Cow" 2:106)

Judaism was concerned with setting the basic principles of behaviour in the Old Testament:

You shall not murder. You shall not commit adultery.
You shall not steal. (Exodus 20:13-15)

In the New Testament of Christianity, basic laws are also emphasized and to them are added other moral values, like modesty and compassion:

So when you give to the needy, do not announce it with
trumpets, as the hypocrites do in the synagogues and on
the streets... (Matthew 6:2)

And:

...Love your enemies, do good to those who hate you.
(Luke 6:27)

Basic laws are combined with moral principles and values in the Qur'an:

Allah commands justice, the doing of good, and liberality
to kith and kin, and He forbids all shameful deeds, and
injustice and rebellion: He instructs you, that ye may
receive admonition. (An-Nahl "The Bees" 16:90)

One may find seeming contradictions among holy books, such as the Old Testament law of:

> ... *life for life, eye for eye, tooth for tooth, hand for hand, foot for foot.* (Deuteronomy 19:21)

and the New Testament admonition:

> *If someone strikes you on the right cheek, turn to him the other.* (Matthew 5:39)

In a demonstration of how old rules are integrated over time, the Qur'an explains that punishment and forgiveness are not mutually exclusive:

> *The recompense for an injury is an injury equal thereto (in degree): but if a person forgives and makes reconciliation, his reward is due from Allah: for (Allah) loveth not those who do wrong.* (Ash-Shura "The Counsel" 42:40)

Acceptance of others

Anyone who reads the Qur'an thoroughly will be guided to

accept others both in principle and in terms of behaviour. On the level of principle, Muslims are instructed to accept others with all their differences, regardless of religion, race, gender or color. On the level of day-to-day behaviour, acceptance is often expressed through forgiveness.

Commonality of humankind

In the Qur'an, God explains that all human beings are of a common origin and that He holds them in particular esteem:

> We have honoured the sons of Adam; provided them with transport on land and sea; given them for sustenance things good and pure; and conferred on them special favours, above a great part of our creation. (Al-'Isrā' "The Night Journey" 17:70)

God is described as compassionate and merciful to all people without discrimination:

> ... For Allah is to all people Most surely full of kindness, Most Merciful. (Al-Baqarah "The Cow" 2:143)

The term "people" refers to all of humankind, which is accountable before God, and instructed to worship Him:

> *O ye people! Adore your Guardian-Lord, who created you and those who came before you, that ye may have the chance to learn righteousness;* (Al-Baqarah "The Cow" 2:21)

And every individual represents all of humankind, regardless of religion, race, or color:

> *... if any one slew a person ... it would be as if he slew the whole people: and if any one saved a life, it would be as if he saved the life of the whole people.* (Al-Ma'idah "The Food" 5:32)

All people were united as one nation in the beginning:

> *Mankind was one single nation, and Allah sent Messengers with glad tidings and warnings; and with them He sent the Book in truth, to judge between people in matters wherein they differed;* (Al-Baqarah "The Cow" 2:213)

They eventually differentiated themselves into separate nations:

> *Mankind was but one nation, but differed (later). Had it not been for a word that went forth before from thy Lord, their differences would have been settled between them.* (Yunus, "Jonas" 10:19)

This differentiation was God's will:

> *If thy Lord had so willed, He could have made mankind one people: but they will not cease to dispute.* (Hud "Hud" 11:118)

God emphasized that such differences among people are for learning about one another, not for creating divisiveness:

> *O mankind! We created you from a single (pair) of a male and a female, and made you into nations and tribes, that ye may know each other (not that ye may despise (each other). Verily the most honoured of you in the sight of Allah is (he who is) the most righteous of you. And Allah has full knowledge and is well acquainted*

(with all things) (Al-Hujurat "The Apartments" 49:13)

He instructed people to honor their parents even if they follow a different religion:

> *And We have enjoined on man (to be good) to his parents: in travail upon travail did his mother bear him, and in years twain was his weaning: (hear the command), "Show gratitude to Me and to thy parents: to Me is (thy final) Goal.*
>
> *"But if they strive to make thee join in worship with Me things of which thou hast no knowledge, obey them not; yet bear them company in this life with justice (and consideration), and follow the way of those who turn to me (in love): in the end the return of you all is to Me, and I will tell you the truth (and meaning) of all that ye did."* (Luqman "Luqman" 31:14-15)

In the story of David and Goliath, the Qur'an gives an example of how God put different kinds of people on earth together to bring balance:

By Allah's will they routed them; and David slew Goliath; and Allah gave him power and wisdom and taught him whatever (else) He willed. And did not Allah check one set of people by means of another, the earth would indeed be full of mischief: But Allah is full of bounty to all the worlds. (Al-Baqarah "The Cow" 2:251)

The rise and fall of nations and individuals over time is God's way of teaching his people not to fall into the trap of assuming superiority. All situations are bound to change:

If a wound hath touched you, be sure a similar wound hath touched the others. Such days (of varying fortunes) We give to men and men by turns: that Allah may know those that believe... (Al-'Imran "The Family of Al-Imran" 3:140)

And God promises that heaven will be the ultimate home of those who are virtuous and not pretentious:

That Home of the Hereafter We shall give to those who intend not high-handedness or mischief on earth: and the end is (best) for the righteous. (Al-Qasas "The Narrative" 28:83)

Forgiveness as acceptance in action

In terms of day-to-day behavior among individuals, the exact words "acceptance of others" do not occur in the Qur'an. However, the Qur'an encourages forgiveness, which is synonymous with accepting others. The word "forgiveness" and its derivatives occur 27 times throughout the Qur'an.

God is generous with forgiveness:

> ... *Allah knoweth what ye used to do secretly among yourselves; but He turned to you and forgave you...* (Al-Baqarah "The Cow" 2:187)

He forgives people their past mistakes:

> ...*Allah forgives what is past...* (Al-Ma'idah "The Food" 5:95)

He grants total forgiveness:

...But Allah Has blotted out (their fault): For Allah is Oft-Forgiving, Most Forbearing. (Al-'Imran "The Family of Al-Imran" 3:155)

Man has the right to retaliate, but the Qur'an urges him to forgive once his right is proven:

The recompense for an injury is an injury equal thereto (in degree): but if a person forgives and makes reconciliation, his reward is due from Allah: for (Allah) loveth not those who do wrong. (Ash-Shura "Counsel" 42:40)

Forgiveness is equated with God's way of relating to people:

...But if ye forgive and overlook, and cover up (their faults), verily Allah is Oft-Forgiving, Most Merciful. (At-Taghabun "The Manifestation of Losses" 64:14)

And God so values mercy that He instructed Prophet Mohamed to pardon others and to ask His forgiveness for them:

It is part of the Mercy of Allah that thou dost deal gently with them Wert thou severe or harsh-hearted, they would have broken away from about thee: so pass over (Their faults), and ask for (Allah's) forgiveness for them… (Al-'Imran "The Family of Al-Imran" 3:159)

Dialogue

The Qur'an states that differences among people are part of God's design, and in order for people to co-exist they must communicate. A strong basis for communication is the common origin of all monotheistic religions and their holy books, as well as the common conviction that only God has the right to judge.

Mutual understanding among religions

The Qur'an stresses the necessity of dialogue among people with the aim of reaching mutual understanding, as opposed to coercion. This is particularly emphasized as it relates to religious conversion.

In this context of striving for mutual understanding, God commands Prophet Mohamed (and the Muslims after him) to seek common ground with the followers of the other monotheistic religions. Their dialogue should be based upon an agreement to worship only one God:

> Say: "O People of the Book! come to common terms as between us and you: That we worship none but Allah; that we associate no partners with him; that we erect not, from among ourselves, Lords and patrons other than Allah." If then they turn back, say ye: "Bear witness that we (at least) are Muslims (bowing to Allah's Will). (Al-'Imran "The Family of Al-Imran" 3:64)

In the eyes of God, Muslims, Jews and Christians are at the same level, as they are all monotheists. They share the same core beliefs and will receive the same reward if they are righteous:

> Those who believe (in the Qur'an), and those who follow the Jewish (scriptures), and the Christians and the Sabians,- any who believe in Allah and the Last Day, and work righteousness, shall have their reward with their Lord; on them shall be no fear, nor shall they grieve. (Al-Baqarah "The Cow" 2:62)

Because each successive monotheistic religion affirms the previous one, and each of the holy books complements the others, there is no reason to coerce any People of the Book. According to the Qur'an, all religions are from God:

> *Say ye: "We believe in Allah, and the revelation given to us, and to Abraham, Isma'il, Isaac, Jacob, and the Tribes, and that given to Moses and Jesus, and that given to (all) prophets from their Lord: We make no difference between one and another of them: And we bow to Allah (in Islam)."* (Al-Baqarah "The Cow" 2:136)

Diversity of belief is God's will

All people are instructed to discuss religious differences graciously and with respect:

> *Invite (all) to the Way of thy Lord with wisdom and beautiful preaching; and argue with them in ways that are best and most gracious: for thy Lord knoweth best, who have strayed from His Path, and who receive guidance..."* (An-Nahl "The Bees" 16:125)

And they are all are reminded that diversity in doctrine and belief is the will of God:

> *If it had been thy Lord's will, they would all have believed,- all who are on earth! wilt thou then compel mankind, against their will, to believe! (Yunus* "Jonas" 10:99)

Therefore, conversations about religion should never be used to force others, or even to try to convince them, to forsake their doctrine. This concept is presented so often throughout the Qur'an that it cannot adequately be contained in a few lines. A representative example is:

> *Let there be no compulsion in religion: Truth stands out clear from Error: whoever rejects evil and believes in Allah hath grasped the most trustworthy hand-hold, that never breaks. And Allah heareth and knoweth all things.* (Al-Baqarah "The Cow" 2:256)

Regardless of the religion or holy book that a person follows, only God has the authority to determine consequences for actions, to judge doctrines as right or wrong, and to judge actions as good or evil. He will decide all on Judgment Day:

> *Those who believe (in the Qur'an), those who follow the Jewish (scriptures), and the Sabians, Christians, Magians, and Polytheists,- Allah will judge between them on the Day of Judgment: for Allah is witness of all things.* (Al-Hajj "The Pilgrimage" 22:17)

Not even the prophets of God had the authority to judge people:

> *Therefore do thou give admonition, for thou art one to admonish. Thou art not one to manage (men's) affairs.* (Al-Ghashiyah "The Overwhelming Event" 88:21-22)

The prophets came only to inform and remind mankind of the truth:

> *The Messenger's duty is but to proclaim (the message). But Allah knoweth all that ye reveal and ye conceal.* (Al-Ma'idah "The Food" 5:99)

Peace

Peace is one of the most fundamental values in Islam. The word 'peace' appears 67 times in the Qur'an and is used to guide relations between God and humans, between Muslims and People of the Book and among people in heaven.

According to the Qur'an, when one submits to God, one chooses peace over war and agrees to seek harmony in transactions with all others, regardless of their religion. Even in conflict, attainment of justice is not a final destination. Peace is always the objective.

Respect and humility

The Qur'an contains instructions meant to maintain peaceful relationships within the human community:

> When a (courteous) greeting is offered you, meet it with a greeting still more courteous, or (at least) of equal courtesy. Allah takes careful account of all things. (An-Nisa' "The Women" 4:86)

And peace is given as one of the names of God:

Allah is He, than Whom there is no other god;- the Sovereign, the Holy One, the Source of Peace (and Perfection)... (Al-Hashr "The Banishment" 59:23)

God describes the night that the Qur'an was revealed to Prophet Mohamed as a night of peace:

Peace!...This until the rise of morn! (Al-Qadr "The Majesty" 97:5)

Muslims are instructed to greet all believers with peace:

When those come to thee who believe in Our signs, Say: "Peace be on you: Your Lord hath inscribed for Himself (the rule of) mercy: verily, if any of you did evil in ignorance, and thereafter repented, and amend (his conduct), lo! He is Oft-forgiving, Most Merciful. (Al-An'am "The Cattle" 6:54)

When angels visited Prophet Abraham in human form, he greeted them with peace and took care of them, even thought he had no idea who they were:

> *There came Our messengers to Abraham with glad tidings. They said, "Peace!" He answered, "Peace!" and hastened to entertain them with a roasted calf.* (Hud "Hud" 11:69)

If someone is speaking nonsense, the Qur'an teaches Muslims to ignore them and wish them peace:

> *And when they hear vain talk, they turn away therefrom and say: "To us our deeds, and to you yours; peace be to you: we seek not the ignorant."* (Al-Qasas "The Narrative" 28:55)

To do so is considered gracious and a sign of humility:

> *And the servants of (Allah) Most Gracious are those who walk on the earth in humility, and when the ignorant address them, they say, "Peace!"* (Al-Furqan "The Discrimination" 25: 63)

Divine guidance is likened to the ways of peace:

Wherewith Allah guideth all who seek His good pleasure to ways of peace and safety, and leadeth them out of darkness, by His will, unto the light,- guideth them to a path that is straight. (Al-Ma'idah "The Food" 5:16)

God rewards believers with eternal life in heaven, which is called the 'Home of Peace'.

But Allah doth call to the Home of Peace: He doth guide whom He pleaseth to a way that is straight. (Yunus "Jonas" 10:25)

Because the relationship among people in heaven is based on peace:

(This will be) their cry therein: "Glory to Thee, O Allah." And "Peace" will be their greeting therein! (Yunus "Jonas" 10:10)

Prophets of peace

The quality of peace predominates in the Qur'an whenever God recounts the deeds of previous prophets. In the narration of the story of Jesus, emphasis is placed on the peace that was on him. In the sura of his mother Mary (Maryam) Jesus says:

> *"So peace is on me the day I was born, the day that I die, and the day that I shall be raised up to life (again)"!*
> (Maryam "Mary" 19:33)

When the flood water dries, God invites Noah and his companions to come down from the ark in peace:

> *The word came: "O Noah! Come down (from the Ark) with peace from Us, and blessing on thee and on some of the peoples (who will spring) from those with thee: but (there will be other) peoples to whom We shall grant their pleasures (for a time), but in the end will a grievous penalty reach them from Us.*
> (Hud "Hud" 11:48)

As Moses and his brother Aaron prepare to approach

Pharaoh, God instructs them to tell Pharaoh that peace will come to him if he releases the Israelites:

> *"So go ye both to him, and say, 'Verily we are messengers sent by thy Lord: Send forth, therefore, the Children of Israel with us, and afflict them not: with a Sign, indeed, have we come from thy Lord! and peace to all who follow guidance!"* (Ta-Ha "Ta-Ha" 20:47)

Conflict and resolution

In times of conflict, the Qur'an instructs Muslims to extend their hands in peace to all who accept or ask for it:

> *But if the enemy incline towards peace, do thou (also) incline towards peace, and trust in God: for He is One that heareth and knoweth (all things).* (Al-Anfal "Voluntary Gifts" 8:61)

If either party in a conflict asks for peace, the other must accept:

> *… Therefore if they withdraw from you but fight you not, and (instead) send you (Guarantees of) peace, then*

God Hath opened no way for you (to war against them).
(An-Nisa' "The Women" 4:90)

And if one party continues with the aggression, self-defense is permitted, but not to exceed the level of the original assault. Ultimately, reconciliation is the best solution:

> *The recompense for an injury is an injury equal thereto (in degree): but if a person forgives and makes reconciliation, his reward is due from Allah: for (Allah) loveth not those who do wrong.* (Ash-Shura "Counsel" 42:40)

Peace is the dream for which all people yearn. It is humanity's most far-reaching goal. All monotheistic religions call for peace and urge their people to work for it. With such commitment, the path of accepting others and of entering into dialogue with the aim of understanding should inevitably lead to peace.

Conclusion

This brief review of verses from the Qur'an demonstrates clearly that working for peace; using dialogue to reach agreements; and accepting others are values fundamental to Islam. The Qur'an illustrates these themes repeatedly as it calls for all people of faith to coexist peacefully, regardless of their inevitable differences.

Dr. Mahmoud Azab

Advisor to the grand imam of Al-Azhar for interfaith dialogue

Dr. Abdel Moati Bayoumi

Dean of the Faculty of Theology, Al-Azhar University

Contributor Biographies

(in alphabetical order)

Bishop Mouneer Hanna Anis is bishop of the Episcopal / Anglican Diocese of Egypt with North Africa and the Horn of Africa, and president bishop of the Episcopal / Anglican Province of Jerusalem and the Middle East. In 2001, he was involved in the establishment of an agreement for dialogue between Al-Azhar and the Anglican Communion.

Dr. Mahmoud Azab, advisor to the grand imam of Al-Azhar for interfaith dialogue, is a professor of Semitic and Islamic Civilizations at the National Institute of Oriental Languages and Civilizations (INALCO), Paris; and a founding member of the Scientific Council of the Civic Center for Religious Studies (CCEFR), Montreuil.

Dr. Abdel Moity Bayoumi (deceased) was dean of the Faculty of Theology at Al-Azhar University, Cairo. He wrote numerous theological treatises and belonged to the Islamic

Research Academy of Al-Azhar Al Sharif; the Supreme Council for Islamic Affairs in Cairo; and the World Association of Al-Azhar Graduates.

Dr. Aly El-Samman is president of the International Union for Intercultural and Interfaith Dialogue and Peace Education; and co-chairman of the Interfaith Working Group of Project Aladdin. Formerly, he was chairman of the Committee for Interreligious Dialogue of the Higher Islamic Council of Egypt; advisor to the Grand Imam of Al-Azhar for Interfaith Dialogue; and foreign media advisor to President Anwar Sadat.

Archbishop Michael Louis Fitzgerald, a Roman Catholic archbishop, is the former president of the Pontifical Council for Interreligious Dialogue; former Apostolic Nuncio (Vatican ambassador) to Egypt and former delegate to the Arab League. In 1998, he was involved in the establishment of an agreement for dialogue between al-Azhar and the Vatican.

Grand Mufti Aly Gomaa, former grand mufti of Egypt, is a member of Al-Azhar's Senior Scholars Authority and Islamic Research Academy, as well as chairman of the board of trustees of the major Egyptian charity Masr Elkhair. Formerly a professor of Islamic jurisprudence at Al-Azhar University, Gomaa has written more than sixty books on various Islamic issues and was general editor of the Encyclopaedia of Hadith.

Dr. Marie-Laure Mimoun-Sorel is an educator and researcher with a PhD from the Australian Catholic University in the transdisciplinary approach to education. She actively promotes understanding among individuals from different cultures and religions, and in 1994 she contributed to the UNESCO interfaith program that produced the "Declaration on the Role of Religion in the Promotion of a Culture of Peace".

Chief Rabbi David Rosen, former chief rabbi of Ireland, is the American Jewish Committee's international director of interreligious affairs, and honorary interfaith advisor to the Chief Rabbinate of Israel. In 2005 Pope Benedict XVI made Rosen a papal knight for contributions to Catholic-Jewish reconciliation; and in 2010 Queen Elizabeth II made him a Commander of the Order of the British Empire for advancing interfaith understanding.

Rabbi Michel Serfaty, a specialist in Masorah and biblical lexicography, is professor emeritus at the University of Nancy-Lorraine 2; rabbi of the metropolitan department of Essonne and of Ris-Orangis, France; and founding president of the Jewish-Muslim Friendship Society of France.

Chief Rabbi René-Samuel Sirat, former chief rabbi of France, is professor emeritus at University of Paris and University of Jerusalem; vice president of the Conference of European Rabbis; secretary-general of the Foundation for Interreligious and Intercultural Research and Dialogue in Geneva; honorary director of the UNESCO Chair "Reciprocal Knowledge of the Religions of the Book and Teaching of Peace"; and co-chairman of the Aladdin Project's Interfaith Working Group.